FIRST DAY BACK AT SCHOOL

BY

Auntie D

This book belongs to:

Today was my first day back at school and can you believe that Ms. Binns was kinda CRUEL!

She complained that I didn't sit in my seat!

...but I only got up for a minute to speak to Pete...

...then I went over and greeted Dover...

...and played a game of "Super Vacuum Explorer."

Next, I followed Sally to her seat and stayed for a bit cause she is sweet.

It's not my fault that my classroom has a lot to offer...

and that includes my favorite class pet "Grandpa Hampster."

I stopped by his cage and he raced through his maze.

Just then I was headed for
my seat when
"Fighter fish Sam"
asked for a treat...

...after his treat
he went straight
to sleep.

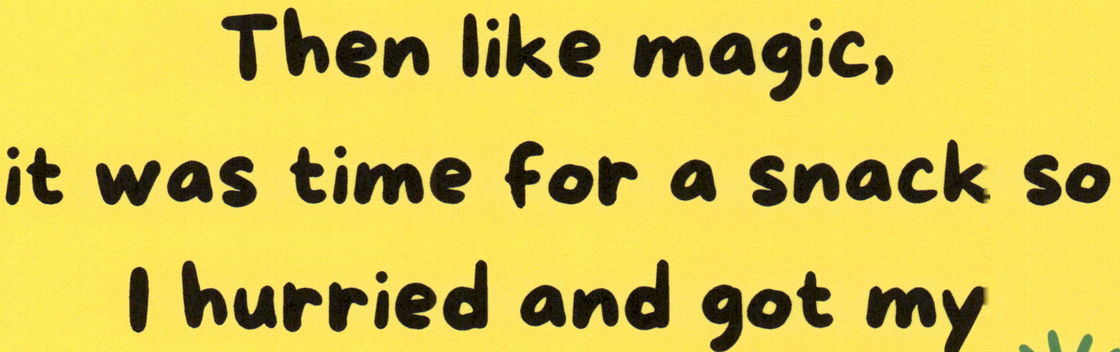

Then like magic,
it was time for a snack so
I hurried and got my
snack pack.

I sat in my seat
and started to eat...

Mmm! Mom had packed
a special treat.

After snack, it was time to play!

...this is what I had waited for all day!

I lined up and waited to go but ...

...my teacher stopped me at the door.

"Wait right here, Tate," she said
"Your playtime will be late!"

"Late! Ms. Binns, but what did I do?"
"I've been a good student through and through."

"Tate Rowe," she said and shook her head...

"Today you behaved a little dread."

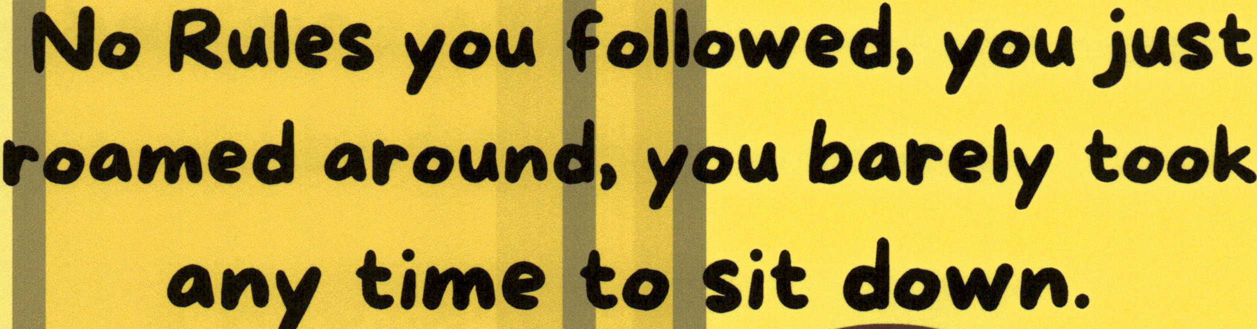

No Rules you followed, you just roamed around, you barely took any time to sit down.

"Ms. Binns," I said and hung my head "I am sorry that I behaved so dread"...

...All I wanted to do was help.

"Tate!" she said and rubbed my head.

"If you really want help..."

" You must learn to follow the Rules! "

"YOU must listen to know what to do."

...then you'll be
a good student
through and through.

www.ingramcontent.com/pod-product-compliance
Ingram Content Group UK Ltd.
Pitfield, Milton Keynes, MK11 3LW, UK
UKHW060115300726
14090UKWH00002B/198

* 9 7 9 8 5 1 2 6 1 8 6 6 0 *